50 Winter Gourmet Dishes

By: Kelly Johnson

Table of Contents

- Beef Wellington
- French Onion Soup
- Lobster Newberg
- Coq au Vin
- Braised Short Ribs
- Duck Confit
- Osso Buco
- Roasted Bone Marrow
- Chestnut Soup
- Veal Parmesan
- Braised Lamb Shanks
- Pot Roast with Root Vegetables
- Roast Pheasant
- Truffle Mashed Potatoes
- Lobster Bisque
- Wild Mushroom Risotto
- Stuffed Squash with Quinoa
- Baked Alaska
- Bouillabaisse

- Venison Stew
- Caviar with Blinis
- Roasted Brussels Sprouts with Bacon
- Pan-Seared Duck Breast
- Caramelized Shallot Tart
- Pumpkin Ravioli with Sage Butter
- Crab Cakes with Remoulade
- Butternut Squash Soup
- Braised Red Cabbage
- Foie Gras with Fig Jam
- Grilled Steak with Red Wine Sauce
- Truffle Risotto
- Roasted Rack of Lamb
- Saffron Risotto
- Braised Pork Belly
- Lobster Tail with Garlic Butter
- Grilled Venison with Herb Sauce
- Stuffed Pheasant with Chestnuts
- Rich Chocolate Mousse
- Roasted Root Vegetables
- Baked Brie with Honey and Almonds

- Mushroom Wellington
- Duck Breast with Cherry Sauce
- Creamy Polenta with Parmesan
- Roast Goose with Apples
- Risotto with Winter Greens
- Chocolate Soufflé
- Smoked Salmon with Dill Sauce
- Spicy Hot Chocolate
- Sautéed Foie Gras with Pears
- Apple Cider Glazed Pork Tenderloin

Beef Wellington

Ingredients:

- 2 lb beef tenderloin, trimmed
- 2 tbsp olive oil
- Salt and pepper, to taste
- 2 tbsp Dijon mustard
- 8 oz cremini mushrooms, finely chopped
- 2 tbsp butter
- 2 tbsp fresh thyme, chopped
- 1/4 cup brandy (optional)
- 1/2 lb puff pastry, thawed
- 1 egg, beaten

Instructions:

1. Preheat the oven to 400°F (200°C).
2. Season the beef tenderloin with salt and pepper. Heat olive oil in a skillet and sear the beef on all sides until browned, about 2-3 minutes per side.
3. Remove the beef and brush with Dijon mustard.
4. In the same skillet, melt butter and sauté mushrooms and thyme until the mushrooms release their moisture and the mixture is dry, about 5 minutes.
5. Optional: Add brandy and cook for another 2 minutes.
6. Lay out a sheet of plastic wrap, place the mushroom mixture on it, and roll the beef into the mixture. Chill for 30 minutes.
7. Roll out puff pastry on a floured surface. Place the beef in the center and wrap it in the pastry. Brush with beaten egg.

8. Bake for 25-30 minutes or until the pastry is golden and the beef reaches the desired doneness.

9. Let rest for 10 minutes before slicing and serving.

French Onion Soup

Ingredients:

- 4 large onions, thinly sliced
- 2 tbsp butter
- 2 tbsp olive oil
- 2 cloves garlic, minced
- 1 tsp sugar
- 1/4 cup white wine
- 6 cups beef broth
- 1 bay leaf
- 2 sprigs thyme
- Salt and pepper, to taste
- 6 slices French baguette
- 2 cups Gruyère cheese, shredded

Instructions:

1. In a large pot, heat butter and olive oil over medium heat. Add the onions, sugar, and a pinch of salt, and cook, stirring frequently, until caramelized, about 30 minutes.
2. Add garlic and cook for another minute.
3. Pour in white wine and scrape up any browned bits from the bottom. Add beef broth, bay leaf, and thyme, and bring to a simmer. Cook for 20 minutes.
4. Season with salt and pepper to taste.
5. Meanwhile, toast the baguette slices and set aside.

6. Ladle soup into bowls, top with a slice of toasted baguette, and sprinkle with Gruyère cheese.

7. Place the bowls under a broiler until the cheese is melted and bubbly, about 2-3 minutes.

Lobster Newberg

Ingredients:

- 4 lobster tails, cooked and chopped
- 2 tbsp butter
- 2 tbsp brandy
- 4 egg yolks
- 1/2 cup heavy cream
- 1 tbsp lemon juice
- Salt and pepper, to taste
- 1/4 cup fresh tarragon, chopped
- 2 tbsp lobster roe (optional)

Instructions:

1. Melt butter in a saucepan over medium heat. Add brandy and cook for 1 minute.
2. In a bowl, whisk together egg yolks and heavy cream. Gradually pour the egg mixture into the saucepan, whisking constantly.
3. Cook the mixture on low heat, stirring constantly until thickened, about 5 minutes.
4. Stir in lemon juice, lobster, and tarragon. Cook for another 2 minutes.
5. Season with salt and pepper.
6. Serve in warm bowls, garnished with lobster roe, if desired.

Coq au Vin

Ingredients:

- 1 whole chicken, cut into pieces
- 2 tbsp olive oil
- 1 onion, chopped
- 2 carrots, sliced
- 2 cloves garlic, minced
- 2 cups red wine
- 2 cups chicken broth
- 2 tbsp tomato paste
- 2 sprigs thyme
- 2 bay leaves
- 1/2 lb mushrooms, sliced
- 1/4 cup fresh parsley, chopped

Instructions:

1. Heat olive oil in a large pot over medium heat. Brown the chicken pieces on all sides, then remove and set aside.
2. In the same pot, sauté onions, carrots, and garlic until softened, about 5 minutes.
3. Add red wine, chicken broth, tomato paste, thyme, and bay leaves. Stir to combine.
4. Return the chicken to the pot, cover, and simmer for 1 hour.
5. Add mushrooms and cook for another 20 minutes.
6. Garnish with fresh parsley before serving.

Braised Short Ribs

Ingredients:

- 4 beef short ribs
- 2 tbsp olive oil
- 1 onion, chopped
- 2 carrots, chopped
- 2 cloves garlic, minced
- 2 cups red wine
- 2 cups beef broth
- 2 sprigs thyme
- 1 bay leaf
- Salt and pepper, to taste

Instructions:

1. Preheat the oven to 325°F (163°C).
2. Heat olive oil in a large ovenproof pot over medium-high heat. Brown the short ribs on all sides, then remove and set aside.
3. In the same pot, sauté onions, carrots, and garlic until softened, about 5 minutes.
4. Add red wine and simmer for 5 minutes. Add beef broth, thyme, and bay leaf.
5. Return the short ribs to the pot, cover, and bake for 3 hours, until the meat is tender and easily pulls away from the bone.
6. Remove the ribs from the pot and strain the sauce. Serve the ribs with the sauce.

Duck Confit

Ingredients:

- 4 duck legs
- 4 cups duck fat (or vegetable oil)
- 4 garlic cloves, smashed
- 2 sprigs thyme
- 2 bay leaves
- Salt and pepper, to taste

Instructions:

1. Season the duck legs with salt and pepper.
2. In a large pot, heat duck fat over low heat. Add the garlic, thyme, and bay leaves.
3. Place the duck legs into the fat and cook on low heat for 2-3 hours, until the meat is tender and falling off the bone.
4. Remove the duck from the fat and crisp the skin in a hot skillet for 2-3 minutes.
5. Serve immediately.

Osso Buco

Ingredients:

- 4 veal shanks
- 2 tbsp olive oil
- 1 onion, chopped
- 2 carrots, chopped
- 2 celery stalks, chopped
- 2 cloves garlic, minced
- 1 cup white wine
- 2 cups chicken broth
- 1 can (14 oz) diced tomatoes
- 2 sprigs thyme
- 2 bay leaves
- Salt and pepper, to taste
- 1/4 cup gremolata (lemon zest, garlic, parsley) for garnish

Instructions:

1. Preheat the oven to 350°F (175°C).
2. Heat olive oil in a large Dutch oven over medium-high heat. Brown the veal shanks on all sides, then remove and set aside.
3. In the same pot, sauté onions, carrots, celery, and garlic until softened, about 5 minutes.
4. Add white wine and cook for 2 minutes. Add chicken broth, tomatoes, thyme, and bay leaves.
5. Return the veal shanks to the pot, cover, and bake for 2 hours until the meat is tender.

6. Garnish with gremolata before serving.

Roasted Bone Marrow

Ingredients:

- 4 beef marrow bones
- 1 tbsp olive oil
- 1 tbsp fresh thyme
- Salt and pepper, to taste
- 1/4 cup chopped parsley
- 1 lemon, cut into wedges

Instructions:

1. Preheat the oven to 450°F (230°C).
2. Place the marrow bones on a baking sheet and drizzle with olive oil.
3. Sprinkle with thyme, salt, and pepper.
4. Roast for 15-20 minutes until the marrow is soft and starting to brown.
5. Sprinkle with parsley and serve with lemon wedges.

Chestnut Soup

Ingredients:

- 2 cups chestnuts, peeled and roasted
- 1 onion, chopped
- 2 carrots, chopped
- 2 cloves garlic, minced
- 4 cups chicken broth
- 1 cup heavy cream
- 2 tbsp butter
- Salt and pepper, to taste

Instructions:

1. In a large pot, melt butter over medium heat. Sauté onions, carrots, and garlic until softened, about 5 minutes.
2. Add chestnuts and chicken broth, bringing to a boil. Reduce heat and simmer for 20 minutes.
3. Puree the soup using an immersion blender or regular blender.
4. Stir in heavy cream, season with salt and pepper, and serve warm.

Veal Parmesan

Ingredients:

- 4 veal cutlets
- 1 cup flour
- 2 eggs, beaten
- 1 cup breadcrumbs
- 1/2 cup Parmesan cheese, grated
- 2 cups marinara sauce
- 1/2 cup mozzarella cheese, shredded
- Salt and pepper, to taste
- Olive oil for frying

Instructions:

1. Season veal cutlets with salt and pepper.
2. Dredge in flour, dip in egg, and coat in a mixture of breadcrumbs and Parmesan cheese.
3. Heat olive oil in a skillet over medium heat. Fry veal cutlets for 2-3 minutes per side until golden brown.
4. Preheat the oven to 375°F (190°C).
5. Place the fried cutlets on a baking sheet, top with marinara sauce and mozzarella, and bake for 10 minutes until cheese is melted and bubbly.
6. Serve immediately.

Braised Lamb Shanks

Ingredients:

- 4 lamb shanks
- 2 tbsp olive oil
- Salt and pepper, to taste
- 1 onion, chopped
- 2 carrots, chopped
- 2 celery stalks, chopped
- 4 garlic cloves, minced
- 1 cup red wine
- 3 cups beef broth
- 2 sprigs rosemary
- 2 sprigs thyme
- 1 bay leaf

Instructions:

1. Preheat the oven to 325°F (163°C).

2. Heat olive oil in a large Dutch oven over medium-high heat. Season the lamb shanks with salt and pepper and brown on all sides. Remove and set aside.

3. Add the onion, carrots, celery, and garlic to the pot and cook until softened, about 5 minutes.

4. Add the red wine and bring to a simmer, scraping up any browned bits from the bottom of the pot.

5. Add the beef broth, rosemary, thyme, and bay leaf. Return the lamb shanks to the pot.

6. Cover the pot and transfer it to the oven. Braise for 2-3 hours, until the lamb is tender.

7. Serve the lamb with the braising liquid and vegetables.

Pot Roast with Root Vegetables

Ingredients:

- 3-4 lb beef chuck roast
- 2 tbsp olive oil
- Salt and pepper, to taste
- 1 onion, chopped
- 4 carrots, chopped
- 4 potatoes, chopped
- 2 parsnips, chopped
- 4 garlic cloves, minced
- 2 cups beef broth
- 1 cup red wine
- 2 sprigs rosemary
- 2 sprigs thyme
- 1 bay leaf

Instructions:

1. Preheat the oven to 325°F (163°C).
2. Heat olive oil in a large ovenproof pot over medium-high heat. Season the beef roast with salt and pepper and sear on all sides until browned.
3. Remove the roast and set it aside. Add the onions, carrots, potatoes, parsnips, and garlic to the pot, cooking for 5 minutes.
4. Add the red wine and beef broth, stirring to combine. Return the roast to the pot.
5. Add the rosemary, thyme, and bay leaf.

6. Cover and transfer the pot to the oven. Roast for 3-4 hours, until the beef is fork-tender.

7. Serve the roast with the vegetables and gravy.

Roast Pheasant

Ingredients:

- 2 pheasant breasts or whole pheasant
- 2 tbsp olive oil
- Salt and pepper, to taste
- 2 tbsp butter
- 2 garlic cloves, minced
- 1 onion, chopped
- 1/2 cup white wine
- 1/2 cup chicken broth
- 1 sprig rosemary
- 1 sprig thyme

Instructions:

1. Preheat the oven to 375°F (190°C).
2. Season the pheasant with salt and pepper. Heat olive oil in a skillet over medium-high heat and brown the pheasant on all sides.
3. Remove the pheasant and set aside. In the same skillet, melt the butter and sauté the garlic and onion until softened.
4. Add the white wine and chicken broth, scraping up any browned bits from the pan.
5. Place the pheasant in a roasting pan and pour the wine and broth mixture over it. Add rosemary and thyme.
6. Roast for 25-30 minutes, basting with the pan juices, until the pheasant is cooked through.
7. Serve with the pan juices.

Truffle Mashed Potatoes

Ingredients:

- 2 lbs potatoes, peeled and cubed
- 4 tbsp butter
- 1/2 cup heavy cream
- 1-2 tbsp truffle oil
- Salt and pepper, to taste
- Fresh chives, chopped (optional)

Instructions:

1. Boil the potatoes in salted water until tender, about 15-20 minutes. Drain and return to the pot.
2. Mash the potatoes with a potato masher or hand mixer until smooth.
3. Add butter, heavy cream, and truffle oil, and stir until well combined.
4. Season with salt and pepper.
5. Garnish with chopped chives before serving.

Lobster Bisque

Ingredients:

- 2 tbsp butter
- 1 onion, chopped
- 2 cloves garlic, minced
- 1/4 cup brandy
- 1/4 cup tomato paste
- 4 cups seafood stock
- 1 1/2 cups heavy cream
- 1/2 lb cooked lobster meat, chopped
- Salt and pepper, to taste
- 1 tbsp fresh parsley, chopped

Instructions:

1. In a large pot, melt butter over medium heat. Add the onion and garlic and sauté until softened.
2. Add brandy and cook for 2 minutes. Stir in tomato paste and cook for another minute.
3. Add seafood stock and bring to a simmer. Cook for 20 minutes to blend the flavors.
4. Add the heavy cream and lobster meat, then simmer for 5-10 minutes.
5. Season with salt and pepper to taste.
6. Serve the bisque garnished with chopped parsley.

Wild Mushroom Risotto

Ingredients:

- 2 tbsp olive oil
- 1 onion, chopped
- 2 cups wild mushrooms, chopped
- 2 cups Arborio rice
- 1/2 cup white wine
- 4 cups chicken broth
- 1/2 cup Parmesan cheese, grated
- 2 tbsp butter
- Salt and pepper, to taste
- Fresh thyme, for garnish

Instructions:

1. Heat olive oil in a large pan over medium heat. Add the onion and cook until softened.
2. Add the mushrooms and cook for 5 minutes until tender.
3. Stir in the Arborio rice and cook for 2 minutes, stirring frequently.
4. Pour in the white wine and stir until absorbed.
5. Gradually add the chicken broth, one cup at a time, stirring constantly and letting the liquid absorb before adding more.
6. Once the rice is creamy and cooked to your desired doneness, stir in the Parmesan cheese and butter.
7. Season with salt and pepper, and garnish with fresh thyme before serving.

Stuffed Squash with Quinoa

Ingredients:

- 2 small squash (such as acorn or butternut), halved and seeds removed
- 1 tbsp olive oil
- Salt and pepper, to taste
- 1 cup quinoa, cooked
- 1/2 cup cranberries, dried
- 1/2 cup walnuts, chopped
- 1/4 cup fresh parsley, chopped
- 1 tbsp maple syrup

Instructions:

1. Preheat the oven to 375°F (190°C).
2. Drizzle the squash halves with olive oil, season with salt and pepper, and place them cut-side down on a baking sheet.
3. Roast for 25-30 minutes, until tender.
4. Meanwhile, cook the quinoa according to package instructions.
5. In a large bowl, combine the cooked quinoa, cranberries, walnuts, parsley, and maple syrup.
6. Once the squash is done, fill the centers with the quinoa mixture.
7. Serve the stuffed squash warm.

Baked Alaska

Ingredients:

- 1 pint vanilla ice cream
- 1 pint chocolate ice cream
- 1 sponge cake, cut into slices
- 4 egg whites
- 1/2 cup sugar
- 1 tsp vanilla extract

Instructions:

1. Preheat the oven to 450°F (230°C).
2. Line a bowl with plastic wrap and layer the vanilla and chocolate ice cream, alternating between them. Freeze for 2 hours.
3. Arrange the sponge cake slices on a baking sheet. Place the ice cream on top of the cake, then freeze again for 30 minutes.
4. Whisk egg whites until stiff peaks form. Gradually add sugar and vanilla extract.
5. Spread the meringue over the ice cream and cake, covering completely.
6. Bake in the preheated oven for 3-5 minutes, until the meringue is golden.
7. Serve immediately.

Bouillabaisse

Ingredients:

- 2 tbsp olive oil
- 1 onion, chopped
- 2 cloves garlic, minced
- 2 tomatoes, chopped
- 4 cups fish stock
- 1/2 cup white wine
- 1 tsp saffron threads
- 1/2 tsp thyme
- 1 lb white fish fillets, cut into chunks
- 1/2 lb shellfish (shrimp, mussels, etc.)
- Salt and pepper, to taste
- Fresh parsley, for garnish
- Crusty bread, for serving

Instructions:

1. Heat olive oil in a large pot over medium heat. Add the onion and garlic and cook until softened.
2. Add the tomatoes, fish stock, white wine, saffron, and thyme. Bring to a simmer and cook for 20 minutes.
3. Add the fish fillets and shellfish, and cook until the fish is cooked through, about 5-7 minutes.
4. Season with salt and pepper.
5. Serve the bouillabaisse with crusty bread and garnish with fresh parsley.

Venison Stew

Ingredients:

- 2 lbs venison, cut into cubes
- 2 tbsp olive oil
- Salt and pepper, to taste
- 1 onion, chopped
- 3 carrots, chopped
- 3 celery stalks, chopped
- 4 cloves garlic, minced
- 2 cups red wine
- 4 cups beef broth
- 2 sprigs thyme
- 2 sprigs rosemary
- 1 bay leaf
- 2 potatoes, peeled and chopped
- 1 tbsp flour (optional, for thickening)

Instructions:

1. Heat olive oil in a large pot over medium-high heat. Season the venison with salt and pepper and brown it on all sides.

2. Remove the venison and set aside. Add the onion, carrots, celery, and garlic to the pot, cooking until softened, about 5 minutes.

3. Pour in the red wine and stir, scraping up any browned bits from the bottom of the pot.

4. Return the venison to the pot along with the beef broth, thyme, rosemary, and bay leaf. Bring to a boil, then reduce to a simmer.

5. Simmer for 1.5-2 hours, until the venison is tender.

6. Add the potatoes and cook until they are soft, about 20 minutes.

7. If you prefer a thicker stew, mix the flour with a little water and stir it into the stew. Cook for another 5 minutes.

8. Serve the stew hot.

Caviar with Blinis

Ingredients:

- 1/4 cup caviar (your choice)
- 12-15 blinis (small Russian pancakes)
- 1/4 cup crème fraîche
- Fresh chives, finely chopped (for garnish)

Instructions:

1. Warm the blinis gently in a pan or oven.
2. Place the blinis on serving plates.
3. Top each blini with a small spoonful of crème fraîche.
4. Add a small amount of caviar on top of the crème fraîche.
5. Garnish with chopped chives.
6. Serve immediately.

Roasted Brussels Sprouts with Bacon

Ingredients:

- 1 lb Brussels sprouts, trimmed and halved
- 4 slices bacon, chopped
- 2 tbsp olive oil
- Salt and pepper, to taste
- 1 tbsp balsamic vinegar

Instructions:

1. Preheat the oven to 400°F (200°C).
2. Heat a large skillet over medium heat and cook the chopped bacon until crispy. Remove the bacon and set aside.
3. Toss the Brussels sprouts with olive oil, salt, and pepper.
4. Spread the Brussels sprouts on a baking sheet and roast for 20-25 minutes, until they are crispy and golden.
5. Toss the roasted Brussels sprouts with the crispy bacon and drizzle with balsamic vinegar before serving.

Pan-Seared Duck Breast

Ingredients:

- 2 duck breasts, skin on
- Salt and pepper, to taste
- 1 tbsp olive oil
- 1/4 cup chicken broth
- 1 tbsp honey
- 1 tbsp balsamic vinegar

Instructions:

1. Score the skin of the duck breasts in a crosshatch pattern. Season with salt and pepper.
2. Heat olive oil in a pan over medium-high heat. Add the duck breasts, skin-side down, and cook for 6-8 minutes, until the skin is crispy and golden.
3. Flip the duck breasts and cook for another 4-5 minutes, until the internal temperature reaches 130°F (54°C) for medium-rare.
4. Remove the duck from the pan and let it rest.
5. In the same pan, add chicken broth, honey, and balsamic vinegar. Simmer for 2-3 minutes to reduce the sauce.
6. Slice the duck breasts and drizzle with the sauce. Serve immediately.

Caramelized Shallot Tart

Ingredients:

- 2 tbsp olive oil
- 8 shallots, thinly sliced
- Salt and pepper, to taste
- 1 sheet puff pastry
- 1/4 cup goat cheese, crumbled
- 1 tbsp fresh thyme leaves

Instructions:

1. Preheat the oven to 375°F (190°C).
2. Heat olive oil in a pan over medium heat. Add the shallots and cook, stirring occasionally, until they are caramelized and golden, about 15-20 minutes. Season with salt and pepper.
3. Roll out the puff pastry on a baking sheet.
4. Spread the caramelized shallots over the pastry, leaving a small border around the edges.
5. Sprinkle the goat cheese and thyme over the shallots.
6. Bake for 20-25 minutes, until the pastry is golden and puffed.
7. Serve warm.

Pumpkin Ravioli with Sage Butter

Ingredients:

- 1 package fresh pumpkin ravioli (or homemade)
- 1/4 cup butter
- 8-10 fresh sage leaves
- Salt and pepper, to taste
- Parmesan cheese, for garnish

Instructions:

1. Cook the pumpkin ravioli according to package instructions. Drain and set aside.
2. In a pan, melt the butter over medium heat. Add the sage leaves and cook for 2-3 minutes until the butter is browned and fragrant.
3. Season with salt and pepper.
4. Toss the cooked ravioli in the sage butter until well coated.
5. Garnish with grated Parmesan and serve immediately.

Crab Cakes with Remoulade

Ingredients:

- 1 lb lump crab meat, drained
- 1/4 cup breadcrumbs
- 1/4 cup mayonnaise
- 1 tbsp Dijon mustard
- 1 tbsp fresh parsley, chopped
- 1 egg, beaten
- 1 tbsp lemon juice
- Salt and pepper, to taste
- 1/4 cup vegetable oil for frying

Remoulade Sauce:

- 1/4 cup mayonnaise
- 1 tbsp Dijon mustard
- 1 tbsp ketchup
- 1 tsp hot sauce
- 1 tbsp capers, chopped
- 1 tbsp lemon juice
- Salt and pepper, to taste

Instructions:

1. In a bowl, combine the crab meat, breadcrumbs, mayonnaise, mustard, parsley, egg, lemon juice, salt, and pepper. Form into 8 small cakes.

2. Heat vegetable oil in a pan over medium-high heat. Fry the crab cakes for 3-4 minutes per side, until golden and crispy.

3. For the remoulade sauce, whisk together all the ingredients.

4. Serve the crab cakes with a side of remoulade sauce.

Butternut Squash Soup

Ingredients:

- 1 medium butternut squash, peeled and cubed
- 1 onion, chopped
- 2 carrots, chopped
- 2 cloves garlic, minced
- 4 cups vegetable broth
- 1/2 tsp ground cinnamon
- 1/4 tsp nutmeg
- Salt and pepper, to taste
- 1/2 cup cream (optional)

Instructions:

1. In a large pot, sauté the onion, carrots, and garlic in olive oil until softened, about 5 minutes.
2. Add the butternut squash, vegetable broth, cinnamon, nutmeg, salt, and pepper. Bring to a boil, then reduce to a simmer.
3. Cook for 25-30 minutes, until the squash is tender.
4. Use an immersion blender to puree the soup until smooth.
5. Stir in the cream if desired. Serve hot.

Braised Red Cabbage

Ingredients:

- 1 medium head red cabbage, shredded
- 1 onion, sliced
- 1 apple, peeled and sliced
- 1/2 cup apple cider vinegar
- 1/4 cup brown sugar
- 1/4 tsp ground cinnamon
- Salt and pepper, to taste
- 2 tbsp olive oil

Instructions:

1. In a large pan, heat the olive oil over medium heat. Add the onion and cook until softened, about 5 minutes.
2. Add the cabbage and apple to the pan, stirring well.
3. Pour in the apple cider vinegar and brown sugar, and season with cinnamon, salt, and pepper.
4. Cover and simmer on low for 45 minutes, stirring occasionally.
5. Serve warm as a side dish.

Foie Gras with Fig Jam

Ingredients:

- 4 foie gras slices
- 2 tbsp butter
- Salt and pepper, to taste
- 2 tbsp fig jam
- Toasted baguette slices, for serving

Instructions:

1. Heat butter in a skillet over medium heat.
2. Season the foie gras slices with salt and pepper, then sear them in the pan for about 2-3 minutes per side, until golden brown.
3. Remove from the skillet and set aside.
4. In the same pan, add the fig jam and cook for 1-2 minutes until slightly heated and softened.
5. Serve the foie gras on toasted baguette slices, topped with the warm fig jam.

Grilled Steak with Red Wine Sauce

Ingredients:

- 2 ribeye or filet mignon steaks
- Salt and pepper, to taste
- 2 tbsp olive oil
- 1/2 cup red wine
- 1 tbsp butter
- 1 shallot, finely chopped
- 1 sprig thyme
- 1 clove garlic, minced

Instructions:

1. Preheat the grill to high heat. Season the steaks with salt and pepper.
2. Grill the steaks for 4-5 minutes per side (for medium-rare) or until your preferred doneness.
3. Remove the steaks from the grill and let them rest.
4. In a saucepan, melt butter over medium heat. Add the shallot and garlic, cooking until soft.
5. Add the red wine and thyme, and simmer for 5-7 minutes until the sauce reduces by half.
6. Serve the steaks with the red wine sauce drizzled over the top.

Truffle Risotto

Ingredients:

- 1 1/2 cups Arborio rice
- 4 cups chicken or vegetable broth
- 1/2 cup white wine
- 1 small onion, finely chopped
- 2 tbsp olive oil
- 1/4 cup Parmesan cheese, grated
- 2 tbsp butter
- 2 tbsp truffle oil (or truffle salt)
- Salt and pepper, to taste
- Fresh parsley, chopped, for garnish

Instructions:

1. In a saucepan, heat the broth and keep it warm.
2. In another pan, heat olive oil and sauté the onion until soft.
3. Add the Arborio rice and cook for 2-3 minutes, stirring frequently.
4. Pour in the white wine and cook until it's mostly absorbed.
5. Gradually add the warm broth, one ladleful at a time, stirring continuously and allowing the liquid to absorb before adding more. Continue this process until the rice is tender, about 18-20 minutes.
6. Stir in the Parmesan cheese, butter, and truffle oil. Season with salt and pepper to taste.
7. Garnish with fresh parsley and serve.

Roasted Rack of Lamb

Ingredients:

- 1 rack of lamb, trimmed
- 2 tbsp olive oil
- 3 cloves garlic, minced
- 2 tbsp fresh rosemary, chopped
- Salt and pepper, to taste
- 1/2 cup red wine
- 1 tbsp balsamic vinegar

Instructions:

1. Preheat the oven to 400°F (200°C).
2. Rub the rack of lamb with olive oil, garlic, rosemary, salt, and pepper.
3. Roast the lamb in the oven for 25-30 minutes, or until the internal temperature reaches 130°F (54°C) for medium-rare.
4. Let the lamb rest for 10 minutes before slicing.
5. In a small saucepan, combine the red wine and balsamic vinegar, simmering for 5-7 minutes until reduced by half.
6. Serve the lamb with the red wine sauce drizzled over the top.

Saffron Risotto

Ingredients:

- 1 1/2 cups Arborio rice
- 4 cups chicken or vegetable broth, warm
- 1/2 cup dry white wine
- 1 small onion, finely chopped
- 2 tbsp olive oil
- 1/4 tsp saffron threads
- 1/4 cup Parmesan cheese, grated
- Salt and pepper, to taste
- 2 tbsp butter

Instructions:

1. In a small bowl, steep the saffron threads in a little warm broth for 5 minutes.
2. In a large pan, heat olive oil and sauté the onion until translucent.
3. Add the rice and cook for 2-3 minutes, stirring frequently.
4. Pour in the white wine and stir until absorbed.
5. Gradually add the warm broth, one ladleful at a time, stirring constantly until the liquid is absorbed before adding more. Continue until the rice is tender and creamy, about 18-20 minutes.
6. Stir in the saffron-infused broth, Parmesan, and butter. Season with salt and pepper.
7. Serve warm.

Braised Pork Belly

Ingredients:

- 2 lbs pork belly, skin scored
- Salt and pepper, to taste
- 1 tbsp olive oil
- 1 onion, chopped
- 4 cloves garlic, minced
- 2 cups apple cider
- 2 cups chicken broth
- 2 sprigs thyme
- 1 sprig rosemary

Instructions:

1. Preheat the oven to 300°F (150°C).
2. Season the pork belly with salt and pepper.
3. In a large oven-safe pot, heat olive oil over medium-high heat. Brown the pork belly on all sides, then remove and set aside.
4. Add the onion and garlic to the pot, cooking until softened.
5. Return the pork belly to the pot, adding the apple cider, chicken broth, thyme, and rosemary. Bring to a simmer.
6. Cover the pot and transfer it to the oven. Braise for 2-2.5 hours, until the pork is tender.
7. Remove the pork belly from the pot and rest for 10 minutes before slicing.

Lobster Tail with Garlic Butter

Ingredients:

- 4 lobster tails
- 1/2 cup butter, melted
- 3 cloves garlic, minced
- 1 tbsp lemon juice
- Salt and pepper, to taste
- Fresh parsley, chopped, for garnish

Instructions:

1. Preheat the oven to 400°F (200°C).
2. Cut the lobster tails in half lengthwise and remove the meat from the shell, leaving the tail intact.
3. In a small bowl, mix the melted butter, garlic, lemon juice, salt, and pepper.
4. Place the lobster tails on a baking sheet and brush them with the garlic butter.
5. Roast for 12-15 minutes, until the lobster meat is opaque and cooked through.
6. Garnish with fresh parsley and serve.

Grilled Venison with Herb Sauce

Ingredients:

- 2 venison steaks
- Salt and pepper, to taste
- 2 tbsp olive oil
- 1/2 cup fresh parsley, chopped
- 2 tbsp fresh rosemary, chopped
- 1 tbsp garlic, minced
- 1 tbsp red wine vinegar
- 1/4 cup olive oil

Instructions:

1. Preheat the grill to medium-high heat. Season the venison steaks with salt and pepper.
2. Grill the steaks for 4-5 minutes per side, or until your preferred doneness is reached.
3. In a bowl, whisk together parsley, rosemary, garlic, red wine vinegar, and olive oil.
4. Serve the venison with the herb sauce drizzled over the top.

Stuffed Pheasant with Chestnuts

Ingredients:

- 2 pheasant breasts, boneless
- Salt and pepper, to taste
- 1/2 cup cooked chestnuts, chopped
- 1/4 cup breadcrumbs
- 2 tbsp fresh thyme, chopped
- 1/4 cup heavy cream
- 1 tbsp butter

Instructions:

1. Preheat the oven to 375°F (190°C).
2. Season the pheasant breasts with salt and pepper.
3. In a bowl, combine the chestnuts, breadcrumbs, thyme, and heavy cream to make the stuffing.
4. Stuff the pheasant breasts with the mixture and secure with toothpicks.
5. In a skillet, heat butter over medium heat. Sear the stuffed pheasant breasts for 2-3 minutes per side.
6. Transfer to the oven and roast for 15-20 minutes, until the internal temperature reaches 165°F (74°C).
7. Serve the stuffed pheasant hot.

Rich Chocolate Mousse

Ingredients:

- 8 oz dark chocolate, chopped
- 3/4 cup heavy cream
- 3 egg yolks
- 1/4 cup sugar
- 1 tsp vanilla extract

Instructions:

1. Melt the chocolate in a heatproof bowl over simmering water. Let it cool slightly.
2. Whip the cream until stiff peaks form and set aside.
3. In a separate bowl, whisk the egg yolks and sugar until light and fluffy.
4. Stir the melted chocolate and vanilla into the egg mixture.
5. Gently fold the whipped cream into the chocolate mixture.
6. Spoon into serving dishes and refrigerate for at least 2 hours before serving.

Roasted Root Vegetables

Ingredients:

- 2 large carrots, peeled and cut into chunks
- 2 parsnips, peeled and cut into chunks
- 1 sweet potato, peeled and cut into chunks
- 1/2 pound Brussels sprouts, trimmed
- 2 tbsp olive oil
- 1 tsp dried thyme
- Salt and pepper, to taste
- Fresh parsley, chopped, for garnish

Instructions:

1. Preheat the oven to 400°F (200°C).
2. In a large bowl, toss all the vegetables with olive oil, thyme, salt, and pepper.
3. Spread the vegetables evenly on a baking sheet.
4. Roast for 30-40 minutes, tossing halfway through, until the vegetables are tender and slightly caramelized.
5. Garnish with fresh parsley and serve.

Baked Brie with Honey and Almonds

Ingredients:

- 1 wheel of Brie cheese
- 2 tbsp honey
- 1/4 cup sliced almonds, toasted
- Fresh thyme, for garnish (optional)

Instructions:

1. Preheat the oven to 350°F (175°C).
2. Place the Brie wheel on a baking sheet lined with parchment paper.
3. Bake for 10-12 minutes, or until the cheese is soft and slightly melted.
4. Remove from the oven and drizzle with honey.
5. Sprinkle with toasted almonds and garnish with fresh thyme.
6. Serve with crackers or sliced baguette.

Mushroom Wellington

Ingredients:

- 2 cups mushrooms, finely chopped
- 1/2 onion, chopped
- 2 tbsp olive oil
- 1/4 cup fresh parsley, chopped
- 1/2 cup breadcrumbs
- 1/2 cup cream cheese
- 1 sheet puff pastry
- 1 egg, beaten (for egg wash)
- Salt and pepper, to taste

Instructions:

1. Preheat the oven to 375°F (190°C).
2. In a pan, heat olive oil over medium heat and sauté the onions until soft.
3. Add the chopped mushrooms and cook until the moisture evaporates and the mixture is dry, about 10 minutes.
4. Stir in the breadcrumbs, cream cheese, and fresh parsley. Season with salt and pepper.
5. Roll out the puff pastry and spoon the mushroom mixture in the center.
6. Fold the pastry over the mushrooms and seal the edges. Brush with the beaten egg.
7. Bake for 25-30 minutes, until golden brown. Let cool slightly before slicing.

Duck Breast with Cherry Sauce

Ingredients:

- 2 duck breasts, skin on
- Salt and pepper, to taste
- 1 cup fresh or frozen cherries, pitted
- 1/4 cup red wine
- 2 tbsp balsamic vinegar
- 1 tbsp honey
- 1 tbsp butter

Instructions:

1. Preheat the oven to 400°F (200°C).
2. Score the duck skin and season with salt and pepper.
3. Heat a skillet over medium-high heat and place the duck breasts skin-side down. Cook for 6-7 minutes, until the skin is crispy and golden.
4. Flip the duck and transfer the skillet to the oven. Roast for 5-7 minutes for medium-rare.
5. Remove the duck and let it rest.
6. In the same skillet, add the cherries, red wine, balsamic vinegar, and honey. Bring to a boil and simmer until the sauce thickens, about 10 minutes.
7. Stir in butter to finish the sauce.
8. Slice the duck and serve with the cherry sauce.

Creamy Polenta with Parmesan

Ingredients:

- 1 cup cornmeal (polenta)
- 4 cups water or chicken broth
- 1/2 cup heavy cream
- 1/2 cup Parmesan cheese, grated
- 2 tbsp butter
- Salt and pepper, to taste

Instructions:

1. In a medium saucepan, bring the water or broth to a boil.
2. Slowly whisk in the cornmeal and reduce the heat to low.
3. Stir constantly, cooking the polenta for 20-25 minutes, until thickened.
4. Stir in the heavy cream, Parmesan, and butter.
5. Season with salt and pepper and serve warm.

Roast Goose with Apples

Ingredients:

- 1 whole goose (4-5 lbs)
- 2 apples, quartered
- 1 onion, quartered
- 2 sprigs rosemary
- 2 tbsp olive oil
- Salt and pepper, to taste
- 1/2 cup white wine
- 1/2 cup chicken broth

Instructions:

1. Preheat the oven to 350°F (175°C).
2. Season the goose with salt and pepper, then stuff the cavity with apples, onion, and rosemary.
3. Rub the outside of the goose with olive oil and season with salt and pepper.
4. Place the goose in a roasting pan and roast for 2.5-3 hours, basting occasionally with the wine and broth.
5. Let the goose rest for 15 minutes before carving.

Risotto with Winter Greens

Ingredients:

- 1 cup Arborio rice
- 4 cups vegetable broth, warm
- 1/2 cup white wine
- 1 small onion, chopped
- 2 tbsp olive oil
- 2 cups winter greens (kale, collard greens, or spinach), chopped
- 1/2 cup Parmesan cheese, grated
- Salt and pepper, to taste

Instructions:

1. In a large pan, heat olive oil and sauté the onion until soft.
2. Add the rice and cook for 2 minutes, stirring frequently.
3. Pour in the white wine and stir until absorbed.
4. Gradually add the warm broth, one ladleful at a time, stirring constantly until the liquid is absorbed before adding more.
5. Once the rice is cooked, stir in the greens and cook for 2-3 minutes, until wilted.
6. Stir in Parmesan cheese and season with salt and pepper.

Chocolate Soufflé

Ingredients:

- 4 oz dark chocolate, chopped
- 1/4 cup sugar, divided
- 1 tbsp butter, for greasing
- 1 tbsp all-purpose flour
- 2 large eggs, separated
- 1/2 tsp vanilla extract
- 1/4 tsp cream of tartar
- 2 tbsp heavy cream

Instructions:

1. Preheat the oven to 375°F (190°C). Butter and dust two ramekins with flour.
2. Melt the chocolate and 2 tbsp of sugar in a heatproof bowl over simmering water. Stir until smooth and cool slightly.
3. Whisk the egg yolks into the chocolate mixture and add vanilla extract.
4. In a separate bowl, beat the egg whites with cream of tartar until stiff peaks form. Gradually add the remaining sugar.
5. Fold the egg whites into the chocolate mixture gently.
6. Spoon the mixture into the ramekins and bake for 15-18 minutes until puffed and set.
7. Serve immediately.

Smoked Salmon with Dill Sauce

Ingredients:

- 8 oz smoked salmon
- 1/2 cup sour cream
- 2 tbsp mayonnaise
- 1 tbsp fresh dill, chopped
- 1 tsp lemon juice
- Salt and pepper, to taste

Instructions:

1. In a small bowl, combine the sour cream, mayonnaise, dill, lemon juice, salt, and pepper.
2. Serve the smoked salmon with a dollop of dill sauce on top.
3. Garnish with additional dill and lemon wedges if desired.

Spicy Hot Chocolate

Ingredients:

- 2 cups milk (or non-dairy milk)
- 1/4 cup heavy cream
- 1/4 cup unsweetened cocoa powder
- 1/4 cup sugar
- 1/2 tsp cinnamon
- 1/4 tsp chili powder (adjust to taste)
- Pinch of cayenne pepper (optional, for extra heat)
- 1/2 tsp vanilla extract
- Whipped cream or marshmallows, for topping (optional)

Instructions:

1. In a medium saucepan, heat the milk and heavy cream over medium heat until warm, but not boiling.
2. In a small bowl, whisk together the cocoa powder, sugar, cinnamon, chili powder, and cayenne pepper.
3. Add the dry ingredients to the warm milk mixture, stirring until completely dissolved.
4. Continue to heat the mixture until it is hot, but not boiling.
5. Stir in the vanilla extract.
6. Pour the hot chocolate into mugs and top with whipped cream or marshmallows if desired.
7. Serve immediately for a warming treat!

Sautéed Foie Gras with Pears

Ingredients:

- 2 foie gras slices (about 1 inch thick)
- 2 pears, peeled, cored, and sliced
- 1 tbsp butter
- 1 tbsp olive oil
- 2 tbsp honey
- 1 tbsp balsamic vinegar
- Salt and pepper, to taste
- Fresh thyme for garnish

Instructions:

1. In a skillet, heat the butter and olive oil over medium-high heat.
2. Season the foie gras with salt and pepper and place it in the hot pan. Sauté for about 2-3 minutes on each side until golden and crispy.
3. Remove the foie gras from the pan and set aside.
4. In the same pan, add the pear slices and sauté until tender, about 3-4 minutes.
5. Drizzle honey and balsamic vinegar over the pears and cook for an additional 1-2 minutes until the sauce thickens.
6. Place the foie gras back into the pan to warm through for 1-2 minutes.
7. Arrange the foie gras on plates, top with pears, and drizzle the sauce from the pan over the top.
8. Garnish with fresh thyme and serve immediately.

Apple Cider Glazed Pork Tenderloin

Ingredients:

- 1 pork tenderloin (about 1 lb)
- 1 cup apple cider
- 2 tbsp Dijon mustard
- 2 tbsp brown sugar
- 1 tbsp apple cider vinegar
- 1 tbsp olive oil
- 2 cloves garlic, minced
- 1 tsp thyme leaves
- Salt and pepper, to taste

Instructions:

1. Preheat the oven to 375°F (190°C).
2. In a small saucepan, combine the apple cider, Dijon mustard, brown sugar, apple cider vinegar, garlic, and thyme. Bring to a simmer over medium heat and cook for about 10-15 minutes, or until the mixture has thickened into a glaze.
3. While the glaze is cooking, heat the olive oil in an oven-safe skillet over medium-high heat.
4. Season the pork tenderloin with salt and pepper, then sear it in the hot skillet for 2-3 minutes on each side until browned.
5. Once browned, brush the apple cider glaze over the pork tenderloin and transfer the skillet to the oven.
6. Roast for 20-25 minutes, or until the internal temperature reaches 145°F (63°C).
7. Remove the pork from the oven and let it rest for 5 minutes before slicing.

8. Serve the pork slices with additional glaze drizzled on top.

www.ingramcontent.com/pod-product-compliance
Lightning Source LLC
LaVergne TN
LVHW081319060526
838201LV00055B/2363